The Metaphysics of Evolution

Evolutionary Theory in Light of First Principles

By

Fr. Chad Ripperger, Ph.D.

1

Manufactured and published by:

Books on Demand GmbH
In de Tarpen 42
22848 Norderstedt
Germany

Phone: +49 40 5343 3520
Fax: +49 40 5343 3584

www.bod.com
info(@)bod.com

ISBN: 9783848215508

Introduction

Nevertheless, this gift of reason can perform these functions safely and well, only when properly trained, that is, when imbued with that sound philosophy which has long stood out as a patrimony handed down from the earliest Christian ages, and so possesses the authority of an even higher order, because the Magisterium of the Church has carefully weighed its principles and chief assertions, which were gradually made clear and defined by men of great genius, by the test of divine "revelation" itself. Indeed, this philosophy, recognized and accepted within the Church, protects the true and sincere value of human understanding, and constant metaphysical principles-namely, of sufficient reason, causality, and immutable truth.[1]

When one reads about evolution, reference is made to evolution as a theory, a fact, a dogma or even fiction. How one views evolution largely depends on one's philosophical assumptions or underpinnings or, to be more specific, it depends on one's philosophy of

---

[1]Pope Pius XII, Humani Generis, para. 29 (DS 2320/3892).

nature. But very often the philosophy of nature is founded on a particular metaphysics and even the empirical sciences have metaphysical underpinnings. Unfortunately, on the side of some scientists, there is a psychological refusal to accept that evolution is not really a conclusion derived from the empirical sciences but really a philosophical theory. Even though most forms of evolutionary theory are really metaphysical considerations, admission of this fact is rare because to admit it means, in the mind of most scientists, that evolution is not scientific. This is based upon the fact that most scientists labor under the belief that the only form of science is an empirical science.

Most empirical scientists assume that empirical sciences are the only valid forms of science because of the fact that their methodology allows for verification, while the other sciences do not. However, the empirical method is not the only valid method of proceeding for a science. While the empirical method is proper to its own material and formal object,[2] it is not proper to philosophy which is also a valid science. Very often, those working in the empirical sciences try to reformulate the definition of a science in order to exclude philosophy (and theology) from being

_____

[2]For a discussion of the material object, formal object and method of the sciences, see Ripperger, *Introduction to the Science of Mental Health*, p 2-12. Certain parts of this text are taken from *Introduction to the Science of Mental Health*.

considered sciences. However, such a motion on their part is inherently contradictory, for the formulation of the definition of a science cannot be derived by the empirical method and therefore to give a true, formal definition requires one to engage in philosophy. So either empirical scientists accept that philosophy is a science or they are left with the unseemly prospect of not having a "scientific" definition of science itself. This is said in order to make clear that to enter into a philosophical discussion about the nature of evolution is a scientific approach, albeit not an empirical one.

The scope and purpose of this work is to place evolutionary theory under philosophical analysis. The reader will note that there will be very little said about the theological question regarding evolution[3] as well as the empirical evidence that mounts day by day which undermines evolutionary theory.[4] Very little has been written on the philosophy of evolution and therefore this book will address certain aspects of metaphysics which are incompatible with various forms of evolutionary theory.

---

[3]For consideration of the theological considerations of evolution, see among others, the website: http://www.kolbecenter.org/.

[4]Numerous texts available both in book form as well as on the internet provide ample evidence in this regard. Any cursory internet search will provide the reader with numerous texts in this regard.

Since the Church has repeatedly pointed Catholic philosophers to the philosophy of St. Thomas[5] in order to avoid error[6], it would seem fitting that in proffering an explanation of aetiology, we employ the writings of St. Thomas. The writings of St. Thomas as well as the writings of authors in the Thomistic tradition offer a good foundation for the discussion of the nature of principles themselves as well as an outline of the various principles. Since not all of the principles would apply to the consideration and discussion of evolutionary theory, we will only focus on a few of those which offer some insight into the difficulties inherent in evolutionary theory.[7]

---

[5]See among others see: Leo XIII, *Aeterni Patris*, passim, but especially paras. 21, 25 and 33; Pope St. Pius X, *Pascendi Dominici Gregis*, para. 45; CIC/83 can. 252, §3 and Sacred Congregation For Catholic Education, *Ratio Fundamentalis*, paras. 79 and 86.

[6]Among other see: Leo XIII, op. cit., paras. 18, 21 & 29 and Pope St. Pius X, loc. cit.

[7]It may behoove the reader to familiarize himself with the terms in the lexicon before reading this text, if he does not possess a scholastic/philosophical training.

Chapter 1:
First Principles

First principles are studied in first philosophy which is a branch of metaphysics.[8] As with any philosophical consideration, it is necessary to discuss the definition of certain concepts before one can proceed. The definition of a principle is as follows:

> **Principle, n. 1.** That from which something in some way follows; a being or truth from which being, change, knowledge, or discussion, respectively, starts. **2.** any cause. (For cause is the main type of principle.) **3.** Anything that is in any way first even if it has no connection with later members.[9]

There are different kinds of principles given the definition. There are some principles which follow from other principles but those principles which are first are those which do not come from another principle and which have no prior principles in their own series.[10] To having no prior principles in its own series means that in

---

[8] See Thomas Aquinas, *In Duodecim Libros Metaphysicorum Aristotelis Expositio*, prooemium.

[9] Wuellner, *A Dictionary Scholastic Philosophy*, p. 244.

[10] Ibid.

that category of first principles, there are no other principles prior to that principle.

Some principles relate to being itself, i.e. to real things, while others determine how we know a thing or come to knowledge of a thing. In the order of being, there is what is called a:

> **Real** principle, the principle from which being proceeds; a being from which another being or modification of being proceeds in some way. Real principles include beginning, foundation, origin, location, condition, cause of any type, and elements of composition.[11]

Real principles tell us something about the very nature of being. Real principles are counter distinguished from logical or what are sometimes called gnoseological principles.

> **Logical principle:** (1) a principle of knowledge; a truth from which other truth proceeds; a source of knowledge or a cause of thought. These include definitions, signs, questions, problems, sources of truth, axioms, norms, premises, bases of division, etc. (2) a rule of logic. (3) a methodological principle or rule of

---

[11]Ibid., p. 245.

procedure special to a science.[12]

A logical principle is one that governs how we come to know a thing and logical principles are said to be built into the very structure of our intellect. By virtue of the fact they are built into our intellect by nature they are said to be connatural. Something is connatural which belongs "to a nature and exist[s] in it from its beginning; congenital or innate; not acquired; present in and operating by natural endowment, tendency or need of nature."[13] Something is connatural which is in the very nature of the thing; it is innate or possessed from the very beginning and it is not acquired or added.[14] It is connatural to the human intellect to perform its

---

[12]Ibid., p. 244. A formal principle is one of the basic principles and rules to justify the validity of reasoning, such as the principle of non-contradiction. All formal principles are logical principles but not all logical principles are formal principles. This is due to the fact that a logical principle deals with knowledge in general, whereas formal principles deal with the principles governing logic or reasoning.

[13]Ibid., p. 59.

[14]Sometimes acquired habits and virtues are said to be connatural, as if to indicate that they constitute a second nature. However, they are not connatural in the proper sense, since they are not innate.

operations according to the first principles, e.g. it is contrary to the nature of the intellect to violate the principle of non-contradiction. In the writings of St. Thomas, we see that there are natural habits regarding the first principles of the intellect. These habits are connatural or natural in the sense that they are not acquired but are in the intellect from the beginning. St. Thomas discusses what he calls the natural habit[15] of *intellectus principiorum* or understanding of the [first] principles. It is a natural or innate[16] habit by which we are able to understand the first principles and insofar as it is innate, it is found equally in all men.[17] This habit helps one to grasp or understand those first principles without inquisition or motion of the intellect,[18] i.e. once the terms are grasped and the formulation of the first principle is heard or thought, one immediately knows or understands the meaning and truth of the principle. This natural habit moves the intellect to grasp the first principles immediately, without ratiocination. This means that one

---

[15]See III Sent., d. 23, q. 3, a. 2, ad 1; ST I, q. 58, a. 3; ibid., q. 79, a. 12; ST I-II, q. 51, a. 1 and ibid., q. 57, a. 2 and De Ver., q. 1, a. 12.

[16]II Sent., d. 24, q. 2, a. 3.

[17]ST II-II, q. 5, a. 4, ad 3.

[18]II Sent., d. 3, q. 1, a. 6, ad 2; ibid., d. 24, q. 3, a. 3, ad 2; III Sent., d. 27, q. 1, a. 3, ad 1 and De malo q. 16, a. 5.

does not grasp the first principles as in a conclusion[19] but they are grasped immediately as self-evident.[20]

Since they are self-evident, one must give assent to the first principles[21] as moved by this natural habit. Moreover, it means that one cannot err regarding the first principles,[22] i.e. reason is always right when it grasps the first principles. However, the history of philosophy, the

---

[19]ST I-II, q. 65, a. 1, ad 3. This would indicate that the Cartesian mentality that one must be able to prove something for it to be true cannot stand for two reasons. The first is that the first principles from which all other conclusions are drawn are self-evident, i.e. grasped immediately without proof. One can only show that, if one rejects a first principle, one is left in absurdity. The second is if everything must be proven, the first principles must be proven by syllogistic reasoning and the premises of that syllogism must be proven, etc. *ad infinitum*. The problem is that there would never be a first principle and subsequently never anything after it. The impossibility of an infinite regress regarding principles militates against the Cartesian notion of everything having to be proven. This would apply equally to the empirical sciences as well as to all the other sciences.

[20]I Sent., d. 3, q. 1, a. 4, ad 3; ST I, q. 17, a. 3, ad 2; SCG II, c. 47, n. 3 and De Ver., q. 10, a. 11, ad 12.

[21]ST I, q. 82, a. 2. See also De Ver., q. 15, a. 1.

[22]ST I, q. 17, a. 3, ad 2.

history of man, as well as common sense experience have shown that man does not always act according to these principles or he does not understand them. Some philosophers have denied implicitly the first principles of the speculative intellect in their philosophical discourses.[23] However, there are two reasons why first principles are repudiated. The first is that the person does not understand the terms of the principle and therefore cannot give assent to it because he cannot understand the formulation of the principle since it is composed of terms not understood. The second is that there is something impeding the use of reason. For example, the young cannot make use of the habit[24] because they have not reached sufficient maturity to think abstractly enough to grasp the principles fully. The gravely mentally ill cannot make use of the habit because of reason's inability to function properly. In fact, one of the ways we know someone is mentally ill is by virtue of the fact that they do not act according to first principles, e.g. they

---

[23]For example, Hume in his critique of causality not only denies the principle of causality which is self-evident but he must also deny the principle of sufficient reason and non-contradiction as a result of his rejection of the principle of causality. Hegel, in his dialectic, holds that in the synthesis both contradictories are contained in the synthesis together, thereby indicating that reason gives assent to two things which are contradictory.

[24]ST I-II, q. 94, a. 1, ad 4.

contradict themselves or assert things which violate the principle of sufficient reason. Another impediment is the foolishness of the person, i.e. as Aristotle observes, it pertains to the fool to deny what is self-evident; or we may say a person who denies self-evident principles is irrational.

In addition to being self-evident, first principles are true, necessary and immediate. The first principles are true because they formulate what is actually the case in the objective order of things. They reflect reality and are not theories or hypotheses, nor are they merely noble ideas capable of realization.[25] First principles are necessary in the sense that there would be no basis for any science without them. For without first principles, reality would be rendered unintelligible to us in that they indicate the fundamental structure of reality, i.e. the created world.[26] First principles are also immediate in the sense that they are truths grasped without the help of intermediate notions or middle terms or, as was stated above, without reasoning. The truth becomes immediately known once the terms are grasped and this is called "self evident" or "known through itself" (per se nota).[27]

Why is it necessary to discuss the nature of

---

[25]McInerny, *Metaphysics*, p. 23. See also Gardeil, *Metaphysics*, page 108.

[26]McInerny, *Metaphysics*, p. 23.

[27]Gardeil, *Metaphysics*, page 108.

principles as well as the principles themselves in the context of evolution? The reason is that evolution, if it is true, must adhere to the first principles. Any violation of the first principles renders either the whole or a part of evolutionary theory false. As will become evident, many aspects of evolution are simply incompatible with first principles.

Chapter 2:
Real Principles and Evolution

In order to evaluate evolutionary theory in its various forms, we want to begin considering the first real principles. We will not be discussing all real principles but only those which apply most directly to the analysis of evolutionary theory.

> **1. Priority of act to potency**: act is prior to potency in nature, in excellence, in intelligibility. Hence it is said to be absolutely prior to potency. (Princ. 2)[28]

In the theory of evolution, the existence of a being comes from that which is lower. For example, something without sight through a mutation begets something with sight. Since the faculty of sight is higher than blindness in the order of being, something without sight begets something with sight. This violates the principle of priority of act to potency insofar as that which has sight (act) has a dependency on that which does not have sight (potency) for its existence. In this

---

[28]All formulations of principles are taken from Wuellner, *Summary of Scholastic Principles,* unless otherwise noted. In this text, we will simply place the principle number as it appears in Wuellner after the principle for reference.

respect, the theory of evolution places potency prior to act, not just in the order of time, but in the ontological order. This however is absurd since to possess a perfection (act) is better than not to have a perfection (potency).

2. **Actualization of potency**: no potency can actualize itself. A potency can be brought to actuality only by the influence of a being in act. (Princ. 5)

While the theory of evolution in part deals with the development of living things from inorganic material, it is often rooted in a cosmological theory of the Big Bang. Some of those who support the Big Bang theory also argue that there is no need for God to account for the Big Bang. For example, Stephen Hawking made headlines by observing, "Spontaneous creation is the reason there is something rather than nothing, why the Universe exists, why we exist. It is not necessary to invoke God to ... set the Universe going."[29] Spontaneous creation is one in which there is no antecedent cause in which the thing simply comes into being from nothing. This violates the principle of the actualization of potency. It is clearly rooted in the principle of sufficient reason as well, which will be dealt with later.

---

[29]Steven Hawkings as quoted in: http://www.huffingtonpost.com/2010/09/02/stephen-hawking-god-not-n_n_703179.html.

In the case of evolution, a particular being which is only potentially capable of begetting another being actualizes itself into a being able to beget a being that is higher than itself. In other words, something which only potentially has sight must actually have sight, at least virtually,[30] in order to give it. Putting aside the question of theistic evolution which we shall address in our discussion of another principle, barring the intervention of a being that has sufficient act in order to beget sight in the order of material causes, a being would have to actualize itself to having an actuality in order to be able to reduce the potency to act, prior to its reducing the other being from potency to act. But this is manifestly not the case. For we notice in the order of causes that nothing can reduce something from potency to act unless it already has that act.[31]

3. **Degrees of being**: a thing is perfect to the degree that it is in act, and imperfect insofar as it

---

[30]Virtually is defined as: "not actually or formally, but equivalently, implicitly, efficaciously, and sometimes, even eminently" (Wuellner, *A Dictionary of Scholastic Philosophy*, p. 322).

[31]We will put aside the question of the actual observability of one species changing into another as indicated by the fossil records. That pertains more to an actual question of empirical science.

is in potency. (Princ. 23)

Variant: The principle of degrees or grades of being: a thing is perfect to the degree that it is in act, and imperfect insofar as it is in potency. (Princ. 209)

Corollary: in material and living bodies we find an ascending order of perfection in which the higher beings have their own perfections as well as those of the lower level of being. In the unity of the higher being the multiplicity of the lower beings is virtually present. (Princ. 210)

Corollary: the principle of continuity: the order of the universe displays a gradual scale of perfections from end to end through all essentially different intermediate steps. (Princ. 212)

In this particular set of principles, what is being stated is that there are degrees of perfection based upon the degrees of act various things possess. The various beings with various degrees of perfection constitute what is known as the hierarchy of being. In the *Summa Contra Gentiles*, St. Thomas Aquinas makes the following observation:

Again, not all creatures are constituted in one level of goodness. For some of them, substance is their form and their act: this is so for that which, because of what it is essentially, it suits to be in act and to be good. For others, indeed, substance is composed of matter and form: to such a being it is suits to be and to be good—but by virtue of some part of it, viz. by virtue of its form. Therefore, divine substance is its own goodness, but a simple substance participates in goodness by virtue of what it is essentially, while composite substance does so by virtue of something that belongs to it as a part.[32]

In the subsequent paragraphs, St. Thomas goes on to discuss the various grades of being within this hierarchy, i.e. there is a being which is perfectly simple

---

[32]SCG III, 20, no 3: Rursus. Non omnes creaturae in uno gradu bonitatis constituuntur. Nam quorundam substantia forma et actus est: scilicet cui secundum id quod est, competit esse actu et bonum esse. quorundam vero substantia ex materia et forma composita est: cui competit actu esse et bonum esse, sed secundum aliquid sui, scilicet secundum formam. Divina igitur substantia sua bonitas est; substantia vero simplex bonitatem participat secundum id quod est; substantia autem composita secundum aliquid sui. (All translations are the authors unless otherwise noted.) See also *De ente et essentia*, chpts. 4f.

whose essence and existence are one (God), beings whose essence and existence are distinct but who are form only (angels) and beings which are composites of form and matter (man and all lower creatures). Even some of the charts that promote evolution, which show different creatures starting from the amoeba going up through various kinds of animals to apes and then finally to human beings, give some indication of this hierarchy. The fundamental problem with evolution is that at root it is a misinterpretation of the hierarchy of being.

Some of the characteristics of the hierarchy of being are expressed by other principles. For example, in the principle of the degrees of material being we find: "in material and living bodies we find an ascending order of perfection in which the higher beings have their own perfections as well as those of the lower level of being. In the unity of the higher being, the multiplicity of the lower beings is virtually present."(Princ. 210) Connected to this is the principle of continuity or the principle of the changes of being which states: "the order of the universe displays a gradual scale of perfections from end to end through all essentially different intermediate steps."(Princ. 212) The universe constitutes a creation[33] in which there is perfection of every grade and level of being from the smallest or most elementary element that exists on its own (for example a single hydrogen atom or

---

[33]The principle of plenitude states: by the free choice of the Creator the universe of being contains all essential levels of perfections and of natures. (Princ. 216)

even some other part of an atom independently existing for short periods of time as we see in certain modern supercollider experiments), all the way up through the various grades of being to God, who is the highest.

A corollary to the principle of continuity or we may say an alternate form of expressing it is: "every superior nature in its least perfection or operation borders on the highest perfection or operation of the nature ranking next below it in the scale of being."(Princ. 214) If one connects these principles indicating the hierarchy of being and its constituent structure, along with the other things which we will be discussing in this book, to the principle which states: "the inference from possibility of being or action to actual being or action is not valid" (Princ. 25), what one discovers is an invalid inference on the side of those proposing evolution. In other words, by looking at the fossil records and considering the hierarchy of being, they infer that lower beings were the cause of higher beings, rather than merely bordering them in the hierarchy of being. Again, putting aside any consideration of whether the fossil records actually contained evidence of macroevolution,[34]

---

[34]Macroevolution is defined as "evolution on a large scale extending over geologic era and resulting in the formation of new taxonomic groups." Alternatively, we may say it is the theory of evolution in which a species possessing new organs or functions evolves out of a species that does not possess those organs or functions. This is counter distinguished from microevolution, which

we can simply see the error committed by the evolutionists in relationship to an invalid inference drawn from the hierarchy of being.

4. The principle of non-contradiction:[35] a thing cannot both be and not be at the same time in the same respect or relation. (Princ. 33)

A variant to this principle states: "the same attribute cannot at the same time and in the same being be truly affirmed and denied of the same subject."(under princ. 33) At first, it does not seem as if those who are proposing evolution are contradicting themselves. But there are a few instances in which we actually see evolutionists violating the principle of non-contradiction. We quoted Stephen Hawking. In the same vein, he makes the following observation: "Because there

---

sees changes within a species.

[35] At times this is called the principle of contradiction. Since the name of the principle actually states the nature of the principle, it is more accurate that it be named the principle of non-contradiction, since things do not contradict themselves rather than contradict themselves. However, it should be noted that in many books that deal with this subject, it is sometimes called the principle of contradiction. For a discussion of this different name for the principle, see McInerny, *Metaphysics,* footnote 10, p. 303.

is a law such as gravity, the Universe can and will create itself from nothing." The contradiction is manifest: to state that the universe can and will create itself is contradictory because it must posit the universe in the order of being in order that it may be able to bring itself out of being or from nothing. We may reformulate his statement in this manner: the universe is from nothing. The universe is treated (i.e. action is predicated of it) as if it is a being, whereas nothing is nonbeing and therefore we see the contradiction.

This is a common error committed when insufficient reflection is given to the mode of knowing of human beings in relationship to the "concept of nothing". If a person truly thinks of nothing, then he is not thinking at all. For us as human beings, in order to think of nothing, we must take something and negate it, e.g. we think of blackness (negation of light) or we think of the absence of existing things or matters of this sort. So when someone proposes that something came from nothing, he is thinking of nothing in terms of something, without recognizing the negation or the fact that no thing exists. It is the thing which is negated that is, in fact, on a psychological level, actually treated as if it were something and therefore, for we human beings can easily err by asserting the existence of nothing, because we are thinking of it as a thing, albeit negated in terms of existence.

Do evolutionists commit the same kind of error?

They do by positing something coming from nothing, i.e. they argue that from a lower grade of being, which does not have a perfection, a perfection comes via a mutation or some other mechanism. Strictly speaking, this is not possible due to the principle of sufficient reason, which we will address shortly. Ultimately, in the order of mutations, the only mutation that should arise from any order of lower beings without the intervention of a higher being is a mutation which is lower than the being who is causing the mutation. This would mean that things are not going from a less organized state to a more organized state in something that is complex.[36]

> **The principle of excluded middle**: a thing must either be or not be at the same time in the same respect or relation. (Princ. 34)

A variant of this real principle is the logical principle of excluded middle which states: an attribute must be either affirmed or denied of its (corresponding) subject. Essentially speaking the principle of the excluded middle states that either a thing is or is not. The problem with evolution is that it asserts that a being has a perfection in order to beget something higher than itself through mutation or some similar form of mechanism, while not having that perfection itself. Since a thing

---

[36]The idea that things are going from a less ordered state to a more ordered state or to greater beings is contrary to the law of entropy.

cannot beget what it does not have,[37] at the most fundamental level, evolutionists who purport that one thing begets a higher thing are stating an inherent contradiction as well as violating the principle of excluded middle, which says a thing either has a perfection or does not. If it does not have the perfection, it cannot pass on that perfection. If it does possess it, then it can.

The principle of sufficient reason, ontological formula:

---

[37]See the principle of sufficient reason below.

A) there is a sufficient reason or adequate necessary objective explanation for the being of whatever is and for all attributes of any being.

B)full formula: every being must have either in itself or in another being a sufficient reason for its possibility, actualities, origin, existence and the mode of existence, its essence (nature or constitution), its subjective potentialities, powers, habits, operations, changes, unity, intelligibility, goodness, beauty, end, relationships, and any other attributes or predicates that may belong to it.(Princ. 35)

Alternate: the existence of being is accountable either in itself or in another.

Without a doubt, this principle is the most violated among evolutionary theorists. Starting with the theory of the Big Bang which is sometimes connected to the theory of evolution, insofar as it is considered that all factors necessary to beget life are already present at the beginning of the universe, we reconsider again Stephen Hawking's observation, "Spontaneous creation is the reason there is something rather than nothing, why the Universe exists, why we exist. It is not necessary to invoke God to ... set the Universe going."[38] That there is

---

[38]Steven   hawkings   as   quoted   in http://www.huffingtonpost.com/2010/09/02/stephen-hawking-god-

here a violation of the principle of sufficient reason is clear, for it does not give a true accounting of the actual existence of the universe. Since nothing is actually a case of nonexistence, i.e. there is no existence or no thing existing, then it cannot bring itself into existence. In this particular case, the theory of spontaneous creation leaves the person without an actual accounting of the existence of the universe because the universe itself cannot in itself give an accounting of its own existence nor did "nothing" have existence to account for its causing the universe to exist. In other words: from nothing, nothing comes.

Under this conceptualization, the reason the current universe cannot give an accounting of its own existence lies in the observation made by St. Thomas in his discussion of the five ways to prove God's existence in the *Summa Theologiae*. St. Thomas observes the following in his first way of proving God's existence:

> But nothing can be reduced from potentiality to actuality, except by some being in act, as that which is actually hot, as fire, makes wood, which is potentially hot, to be actually hot, and thereby moves and changes it. Now it is not possible that the same thing should be at once in actuality and potentiality in the same respect, but only in different respects. For what is actually hot cannot

not-n_n_703179.html.

27

at the same time be potentially hot; but it is at the same time potentially cold. It is therefore impossible that in the same respect and in the same way a thing should be both mover and moved, i.e. that it should move itself. Therefore, whatever is in motion must be put in motion by another.[39]

While this is the principle of motion, the formulation here clearly manifests the principle of sufficient reason insofar as a thing cannot render itself into motion or existence because then there would not be a sufficient reason for its motion or existence. The same holds true in relationship to the Big Bang, prescinding

---

[39]ST I, q. 2, a. 3: movere enim nihil aliud est quam educere aliquid de potentia in actum, de potentia autem non potest aliquid reduci in actum, nisi per aliquod ens in actu, sicut calidum in actu, ut ignis, facit lignum, quod est calidum in potentia, esse actu calidum, et per hoc movet et alterat ipsum. Non autem est possibile ut idem sit simul in actu et potentia secundum idem, sed solum secundum diversa, quod enim est calidum in actu, non potest simul esse calidum in potentia, sed est simul frigidum in potentia. Impossibile est ergo quod, secundum idem et eodem modo, aliquid sit movens et motum, vel quod moveat seipsum. Omne ergo quod movetur, oportet ab alio moveri.

from the consideration of a deity, for nothing cannot bring itself into existence because the existence was not there to begin with.

In the context of evolution, we find the same difficulty. Since one species does not have the existence of the essence in itself to be able to confer it to another species, it cannot be the cause of another species/essence. There are two aspects to this consideration. The first is the nature by which a thing acts and the necessity for the essence to be created directly by God. In relationship to the first consideration, all things that are created do not act through their substances[40] (essence/species) but through proper accidents[41] called faculties and so the faculties are those by which a thing acts. These proper accidents or faculties flow from the essence.[42]

At this point, it is necessary to take a slight diversion into epistemology and another area of

---

[40]ST I, q. 77, a. 1; I Sent., d. 3, q. 4, a. 2; Quod. X, q. 3, a. 1; *De spiritualibus creaturis*, a. 11 and *De anima*, a. 12.

[41]A proper accident is an accident which always accompanies a given substance. Whenever a given substance exists, the accident is likewise present.

[42]ST I, q. 77, a. 6 and I Sent., d. 3, q. 4, a. 2. In the case of man, the proper accidents flow from the essence of the soul.

metaphysics.[43] Metaphysicians observe that not any accident can exist in any substance, e.g. thought, which is an accident in man, cannot exist in a stone because the substance of a stone does not have enough act to cause the act of existence of thought. St. Thomas makes the following observations about the relationship of substances and accidents:

As the essence of some universal species is related to all per se accidents of the species, so the essence of the singular is related to all the proper accidents of that singular; all the accidents found in it are of such a kind: since those are made proper to things by virtue of that in which things are individuated. Moreover, the intellect knowing the essence of the species, through it comprehends all the per se accidents of that species: since, according to the Philosopher [i.e. Aristotle], of every demonstration which arrives at a conclusion about the proper accidents of a subject, the principle [i.e. premise] is that which is.[44]

---

[43]The following section is in substance taken from Ripperger, *An Introduction to the Science of Mental Health*, 55-57.

[44]De Ver., q. 2, a. 7: "sicut se habet essentia universalis alicuius speciei ad omnia per se accidentia illius speciei, ita se habet essentia singularis ad omnia accidentia propria illius singularis, cuiusmodi sunt omnia accidentia in eo inventa: quia per hoc quod in ipso individuantur, efficiuntur ei propria. Intellectus autem

St. Thomas is noting that the intellect knows the accidents which relate per se (i.e. essentially) to a specific kind of essence. In other words, certain kinds of accidents reside in certain kinds of substances. Not every accident can reside in every kind of substance. For example, accidents of lead, such as its color, texture, density, etc. cannot be the same as the accidents of a human being. Each has different accidents. Since the substance can only cause certain accidents, only certain accidents can exist in it. The different kinds of accidents relate to the different kinds of substance.[45] This essentially means that a specific set of accidents actually reveals the nature of the substance. For instance, when we observe a stone, we do not observe rational behavior; we do not observe free acts of the will; we do not

---

cognoscens essentiam speciei, per eam comprehendit omnia per se accidentia speciei illius: quia, secundum philosophum, omnis demonstrationis, per quam accidentia propria de subiecto concluduntur, principium est quod quid est." The Latin phrase "quod quid est," translated as "that which is," is a technical Latin idiom in the medieval period referring to the essence of a thing.

[45]In De Ver., q. 27, a. 2, ad 7, St. Thomas makes the observation that the accidents of the soul are proportionate to the soul. This is a sign that there is a fundamental relationship between the kinds of accidents that can exist in certain kinds of substances.

observe speech coming from the stone because these types of accidents cannot exist in a stone. However, the stone does reveal its substance through its accidents, i.e. by virtue of the fact that it has certain colors and textures and consistencies, it reveals that it has the essence of stoneness and not the essence of dogness. The fact that it lies motionless unless it is acted upon from the outside indicates that it is not alive and does not possess a faculty of locomotion. Its rest reveals that it is a stone and not an animal.

This also implies that two essentially different substances are incapable of having the same accidents. For instance lead and gold cannot have the same accidents since they are essentially different. However, this is not to deny that some categories of accidents can be shared by two essentially different substances, e.g. a man with black hair has the same quality of color of hair as a black bear. However, while they may have some accidents in common, they do not have all the same accidents in common, i.e. a man and bear do not have the exact same set of accidents, for a man is bipedal while a black bear is quadrupedal. Moreover, even the hair that might have the same color will reveal that it comes from a bear by virtue of its coarseness, consistency, etc., so that even accidents that are shared are joined to accidents which differentiate the thing that they affect, e.g. even though a bear and a man may have the same hair color, the hair of a bear is accidentally different in other ways from the hair of a man. Hence, the various accidents come together collectively to reveal the essence of a thing. There appear to be three kinds of accidents in relation to essences. 1) There are those kinds of accidents which are *per se* accidents and always accompany a given essence, sometimes called proper accidents since they are proper to an essence as such, e.g. whenever one finds a human essence, one also finds a possible intellect and will. 2) Then there are those accidents which are common to many in a species but not necessarily to all, e.g. man, generally speaking, has hair on his head, but some men are bald. Even these accidents reveal the nature, for as was shown in the example, a bear's hair and man's hair are different. Moreover, the fact that one finds a biped which is bald on the head but has hair elsewhere is found only in men, even though it is not a proper accident. 3) Then there are those accidents which are not common or found in the most part in men, but in a few, e.g. red haired people are not that common in comparison to black or blond haired people. But even the scarcity of the red-hairedness reveals man's nature to a degree because, again, it is coupled with other qualities which other animals do not have and the accidents are a part of the total number of possible types of accidents in relation to the human essence. In other words, even though two substances have the same essence, their accidents may vary, but even those accidents which vary are limited by the nature of the thing. It is not possible for a human essence to have the accidental qualities of hair which are proper to a goat. What this means is that even though a given essence can reveal itself in a variety of accidental variations, those variations are always within a given set of possibilities. But those various accidents in themselves reveal something about the nature, but in different ways, e.g. one person's speech which is an accident may contain a southern drawl but another's may reflect a different accent and yet we know that those two accidents are possible modifications of speech.

Since there is a specific kind of relation between the accidents and the substance, the essence of a thing is implicitly contained in the accidents, for only certain accidents can reside in certain substances. This fact is expressed in the principle of operation, which is expressed as *agere sequitur esse* (action follows upon being) or *operatio sequitur esse* (operation follows upon being).[46] This principle essentially states that the nature of the being determines the nature of the operation or act. In this case, a substance determines the types of accidents or actions.

The reversal of this principle expresses the basis of the cognitive order. While in the ontological order the type of being determines the actions, in the cognitive order, the actions reveal the substance. This is because the human intellect is a mirror image[47] of the ontological

---

[46]See below.

[47]St. Thomas observes that the concept in the possible

order. The ontological order starts first with existence of some thing (essence) in which adhere accidents (existence-essence-accidents), whereas the human cognitive powers first know the accidents, then the essence, then the existence. Abstraction is the process by which the agent intellect draws out the essence which is revealed in the accidents which are contained in the phantasm in the imagination. Therefore, the agent intellect is able to derive the intelligible species by means of induction, i.e. by separating the form which is implicit in the particular accidents of a thing to derive the universal nature or essence of the thing which corresponds to those accidents.[48] It is precisely because the substance expresses or reveals itself through its accidents that the agent intellect is able to derive the essence from those revealing accidents. The process of abstraction which is the process of drawing the essence out of the accidents is analogous to the putting together of the pieces of a jigsaw puzzle. If one took a box

---

intellect is like a mirror image with respect to the thing itself, see SCG II, c. 74, n. 2. While this is observed in respect to the possible intellect, it can be applied to the entire intellect, including the possible intellect, agent intellect, four interior senses and the five exterior senses.

[48]For a greater understanding of this section pertaining to epistemology, see Ripperger, op. cit.

containing the pieces of the puzzle which was not yet constructed, one could not see the picture, even though the entire picture was contained in the pieces. Analogically, the agent intellect is able to "see" the picture (essence)in the pieces (accidents) which contain the picture. The agent intellect is an important faculty. It makes it possible for man to keep in contact with reality since it abstracts the essences of real things from their accidents. It makes it possible for man to have true intellectual knowledge of things by means of his senses.

By holding that one species causes another, the theory of evolution essentially asserts that since a thing acts through its accidents, it is through the accidents of a thing that a mutation either in that thing or from some external cause, such as environment, causes the other thing to have the characteristics that are proper to a different species. But the various essences or substances in the environment do not have sufficient order to be able to cause a mutation of a higher order because, in that particular case, the things in the environment do not contain sufficient existence to be able to beget that existence in another thing. Moreover, the environment cannot cause an essence, for an essence is greater than accidents. This is based upon what is called the principle of the cause is greater than the effect.[49] The fact that the essence confers existence to the accidents and therefore is a cause of the accidents, shows that it is therefore

---

[49]See Wuellner, p. 31, princ. 92.

greater than the accidents. Based upon the principle of sufficient reason, we begin to see that there has to be a proportion between the cause and the effect and since the environment is lower in the order of being than the mutation, it would cause in some species a higher order; there would not be here a proportion between the cause and the effect and thus there is a violation of the principle of sufficient reason.

If we talk about one species causing another, we are left with the same problem. Since each species/essence acts through its accidents, the accidents cannot cause a change of a higher order in some other thing when the causing agent is of a lower order. In other words, one essence acting through its accidents cannot beget another essence of a higher order through those accidents.[50] Metaphysically, evolution without the aid of a deity[51] is intellectually unsustainable at the level of first principles.

What of the objection that evolution is actually not a case of begetting a higher being from one species to another but merely a higher being begetting different abilities on a lower being. This violates the principle of

---

[50]This is the basis for saying that only God can create an essence since only He acts through His substance and therefore can create another substance/essence/species.

[51]Again, we will discuss the aid of a deity in the context of evolution below.

sufficient reason based upon the fact that you cannot give what you do not have. If a particular species does not have the gift of sight, it cannot beget the gift of sight to some other thing based upon the fact that it does not have the existence or sufficient act in itself to create that gift of sight, because it does not possess it in some manner.[52]

Furthermore, it is self evident to human reason that some perfections are higher than others and this is based upon a principle of hierarchy of being, which was discussed above. To have sight is greater than not to have sight or one may say the same thing in relationship to any perfection which evolutionists claim is bequeathed by mutations to lower things. While it is true that some perfections require a greater complexity at the material level, the possession of those perfections is still higher. Moreover, the more complex a thing is, the greater principle of unification is required to have that complexity work harmoniously. Essentially what this means is that the substantial form of a thing must be on a

---

[52]The formulation of this last sentence is very precise. God does not have physical sight in the substance of deity itself, even though we say He is the cause of sight in those things that have it. But this is by virtue of the fact that God contains all perfections in Himself, analogically speaking. For a discussion of that consideration, see ST I, q. 4, a. 3 and SCG I, c. 29.

higher order so that greater complexity can be brought about at the level of matter. In evolution, further complexity in matter is asserted without accounting for higher substantial form. This again violates the principle of sufficient reason.[53]

To return to the question of the relationship between accidents and substance, it was noted that certain kinds of accidents reside in certain kinds of substances. Not every accident can reside in every kind of substance. Since any given substance can only cause certain accidents, only certain accidents can exist in it. Yet, this also means that there are two kinds of substance. There are those kinds of substances which can only have certain accidents and those accidents cannot vary, e.g. hydrogen as an independently existing substance can only have a specific set of accidents and those accidents cannot vary. There are those kinds of substances in which the accidents can vary within a certain gamut, e.g. a human being can have a variety of different colors of skin (color being the accident of

---

[53]Wuellner lists, among others, in his exercises for the principle of sufficient reason, the following things that require a sufficient reason (p. 17): the beginning of a new being; the existence of this contingent universe; variety in the universe; order in the universe; the continuing existence of accidents; life in man; the unity of man's nature.

quality). Even when a particular substance has a specific accident, that accident can vary under certain circumstances, e.g. a man goes out and stays in the sun for long period of time and his skin changes from white to tan. This fact, observable in nature, shows us that when certain kinds of substances are acted upon from the outside, the result can be a variation in the accidents. Most notably, this is seen in fruit flies. This indicates that a particular substance (essence) can undergo accidental change within the context of what that substance is able to support according to its nature. This variation within a species is sometimes called microevolution. Hence, we see that microevolution is possible, while macroevolution is not.

7. **The principle of proportionate causality**: the effect cannot be greater than the cause. (Princ. 87a)

Variant: the cause must possess, at least virtually but not necessarily formally, whatever perfection it gives to the effect. (Princ. 87b)

Variant: activities cannot surpass the perfection of the natures, forms, and powers which perform them. (Princ. 87d)

Variant: The cause always surpasses the effect somehow. The cause is nobler than the effect. That is, the cause of anything is that kind of thing in a greater degree. (Princ. 92)

In the context of evolution, this is somewhat connected to the principle of sufficient reason but it is formally different. In the case of the principle of sufficient reason, there has to be accountability relative to the existence of the thing either in itself or in another. But this principle indicates that an effect cannot have greater existence than the cause. In the case of macroevolution, the higher being (effect) is greater than its cause (environment or some such thing). For example, when something which does not have sight begets a being which does have sight, the effect is greater than what is found in the cause. It is possible to have more than one cause in any given effect. According to some evolutionists, the mutation occurs when one particular being is acted upon by environmental causes or factors and therefore results in a different being. The difficulty lies in the fact that neither the being which is the primary cause nor the environmental causes possess a perfection that they bequeathed to the thing (effect). As with the example of sight, the primary being which receives the causation from the environmental factor or factors does not possess sight. Nor did environmental factors possess that perfection, for if they did, then it is not a true case of evolution. Two or more causes that do not contain a perfection which is higher in the order of existence cannot together produce an effect that is higher than all of them. This precludes one being evolving into a higher being by environmental factors or other agents that do not already contain that perfection.

8. The principle of resemblance: every agent produces a thing that is in some degree like its own form.
Variant: like begets like.
Variant: substance can only come from substance.
Variant: all life comes from life.

This principle is connected to the principle of sufficient reason insofar as each thing which possesses a perfection can only bequeath that same perfection. A thing cannot give what it does not have. But if it has a perfection, it can be the cause of that same perfection. If it does not have a perfection, it cannot give that perfection. In the context of the principle of resemblance, this means that *the nature of a thing determines the nature of its effects*. In the case of macroevolution, beings are bequeathing to others perfections that they do not have and things that are not like themselves. The variant which states that substance can only come from substance indicates that no created thing, since it acts through its accidents, can be the cause of a higher substance. For accidents cannot cause substances because they do not have sufficient existence or act, since accidents are lower in the order of being than substances. This is the foundation for the Scholastics saying that only God (substance) can create (another substance). Moreover, since life is a higher order of existence than nonlife, only that which has life in some analogous way can beget something that has life. The inverse of this principle logically compels the conclusion that inorganic substances cannot produce organic substances, for inorganic substances would just produce other inorganic substances, not organic substances.

9. **The principle of operation**: *agere sequitur esse* (operation follows upon being). (Princ. 97)

Variant: as a thing acts, so it is. As a thing is, so it acts.
Variant: the mode of being determines the mode of operation.
Variant: actions reveal the essence.
Variant: each thing acts according to its own form.
Corollary: activities cannot surpass the perfection of the being (nature, form, power) which is the principle from which these proceed.
Corollary: the acts are like the nature.

Essentially what this principle states is that the nature of a thing determines how it acts or behaves. In the context of macroevolution, what is ultimately asserted is that a particular nature does not act or behave according to its nature, for it is producing something that is not according to its nature. Moreover, since a

43

particular action or behavior of a particular substance reveals the essence, in the case of macroevolution what is being produced does not in fact reveal the nature of the thing. This follows from the fact that what it is producing is different from itself and therefore does not reveal the nature of that substance or nature. Just as the discussion above regarding the accidents and how they must relate to a specific kind of substance indicates that only certain substances can have certain kinds of accidents and therefore act in certain ways (action is an accident in a substance), so in one being causing another, it can only do so according to its nature. This means it is impossible, based upon the principle of operation, for one being to act in such a way that it begets something contrary or different from its nature. This principle limits the action based upon the limits of the essence or nature and therefore makes it impossible for it to beget something higher than itself, greater than itself or different from itself. While in this particular case the connection is similar to the principle of resemblance, the foundation for that is the principle of operation, since like begets like is based upon the principle that a thing can only act according to its nature and therefore produces only something that is like its nature, i.e. the principle of operation. Macroevolution essentially asserts that a thing does not act according to its nature, for if it acted according to its nature, it would not produce something other than its nature. Or to put it another way, the principle of operation coupled with the principle of resemblance indicates one species can only cause its own species or likeness.

10. The principle of uniformity of nature: a necessary or natural cause always produces the same effect, one effect, and always acts with the same intensity and in the same manner. (Princ.107)

Variant: the same natural (necessary) causes under the same adequate set of circumstances always produce the same result(s).

As was mentioned above, inorganic compounds cannot produce life because life does not exist in the inorganic compounds. Even when one has more than one set of causes, if life is not contained in those causes, life cannot come from those causes, regardless of how many there might be. To put this in the context of macroevolution, a "primordial soup and lightning" cannot produce something that has life because neither one of them has it. To state that they do denies the principle of uniformity of nature because it is stating that things are producing enough act that are different from themselves or in a different intensity or in a different manner than those causes possess, rather than the same effect, same intensity and same manner.

11. The principle of finality: every agent or

nature in acting must act for an end. (Princ. 127)

This principle essentially states that any time any kind of activity occurs, there must be a finality for that activity, i.e. contained in every action there is an intrinsic finality towards which that action is striving. In some evolutionary theories, the change in species is due to random mutation. But random change begetting a new species is against the principle of finality since all the agents involved in producing the change in a species would have to be acting according to their natures which would determine what kinds of finality they would introduce into the action. Due to the principle of resemblance, there are, strictly speaking, in the natural order, no random causes but only causes which act according to a definite finality based upon the natures of their actions which flow from their own natures or essences.

All natures of the same species have the same intrinsic end (Princ. 146) and every end is achieved by some means. The end determines the means (see Princ. 134) or action. Therefore, all natures of the same species have the same determinate ends and therefore those determinate ends specify the means that the particular nature is able to employ or, we may say, the particular actions the thing may perform. Yet, form is the end of generation (Princ. 176) and so we must conclude that every being tries to produce its own form (i.e. produce something like itself) in the process of generation.

However, in macroevolution, the thing's own form is not the finality of the action that ends up occurring. When we take the order of causes into consideration, there may be more than one cause and therefore more than one agent may be causing the changes. However, each one of these agents produces its own form in some way in the effects. However, there is nowhere in the agents an introduction of a form which is higher, either by mutation or some other mechanism of this sort. Rather, each agent produces or contributes its own form so that when more than one agent comes together, they produce something that does not have a form that is not like the two of them, or three of them, etc., taken together.

12. **The principle of finiteness of received act**: every act that is finite is limited by the potency receiving it. (Princ. 158)

Essentially what this principle states is that anytime a cause brings about an act in something that has the potentiality to receive that act, that potentiality limits the reception of the act. This is somewhat of a variation of the principle that "whatever is received is received according to the mode of the receiver." (Princ. 378) This is important to keep in mind in the context of evolution because the being receiving actuality from some kind of cause or causes limits the reception of the act that is received. In effect, this means that the particular nature of the thing receiving the actuality limits how the causes can act upon it by virtue of the potentiality within the thing that is receiving the activity.

If we recall the principle of operation which states that a thing acts as it is or that nature determines action or that being determines act, on the side of the cause, there is always potentiality introduced into the effect. Any time a limited thing acts, i.e. a thing which is determined in the finiteness of its being by potentiality, it introduces some aspect of its potentiality into the thing that it causes. In other words, like (potentiality or limitedness) begets like (potentiality or limitedness). Therefore, this principle is the result of not only the principle of operation but also the principle of resemblance, efficient causality, as well as several other principles.

If one takes the principle that every act that is finite is limited by the potency receiving it and consider that a thing introducing its own potentiality in the thing that it causes because the cause is always in some way in the effect, potentiality is always being introduced into the effect and being determined by the effect. In the case of evolution, these two principles are being denied by virtue of the fact that the potency receiving it is actually receiving something beyond which it is capable of receiving and the thing causing is not producing the potency in the effect which it has by nature, for it is causing something greater. For example, if a thing does not have sight, it introduces that limitation into the effect, i.e. lack of sight. If the thing caused does not contain sight or have the capacity for sight, the sight will not be caused. Therefore, on the side of both the limited cause and on the side of the thing caused, there is not sufficient act in order to produce a higher effect.[54]

---

[54]In creation, since God is pure act, there is no potency in Him and therefore He is able, both on the side of the cause (i.e. Himself) as well as on the side of the effect, to produce something which is not restricted in its potency except insofar as it depends upon Him. In other words, God can arrange on the side of the thing caused its potency to be able to receive a particular actualization which He causes. This is why evolution is not possible but creation is.

Chapter 3:
Logical Principles and Evolution

Having discussed the real principles in relationship to evolution, we now turn our attention to logical or formal principles. As was mentioned, a logical or formal principle is one which governs the process of reasoning. The logical principles reflect the structure and nature of the intellect in conjunction with the ontological nature of things. In other words, our intellect has a specific structure and the principles reflect that structure by indicating the proper mode by which the intellect must operate to be true to its proper nature. The human intellect is designed to know ontological reality and therefore the principles that express ontological reality govern the operations of the intellect. In effect, we cannot reason properly unless we follow proper logical principles which adhere to ontological reality. We must therefore ask the question whether evolution properly adheres to logical principles and the best way to answer that question is to simply take a look at a few of the logical principles to see whether it properly adheres to those principles.

1. **The principle of evidence**: the objective evidence of being is the criterion of the truth of assent in the motive for certain assent. (Princ.

155)
Variant: the thing in the condition of evidence is the measure of the truth of judgments.
Variant: there is no argument against the evidence. (Princ. 156a)
Variant: no inference contrary to the fact(s) is true. (Princ. 156b)
Variant: an explanation or hypothesis must take account of *all* the evidence. (Princ. 157)

This principle constitutes a real difficulty for certain scientists who support evolution. There is certain evidence which is incompatible with evolution that has not been adequately explained by the scientists who support evolution. The fallacy that is often committed is called the fallacy of over generalization, in which a person tends to ignore or is unaware of certain things and makes a generalization which appears to cover all of the evidence. The problem is that the principle of evidence cannot be denied.

What proof do we have that certain evolutionists are in fact ignoring evidence contrary to evolution?[55]

---

[55]It should be noted that the point of this book is not to provide the scientific foundation for why evolution is problematic but here we simply provide cursory scientific evidence that pertains to the particular principle being delineated. Any cursory search on the internet will provide ample sources of scientific evidence

There are no transitional links and intermediate forms in either the fossil record or the modern world. Therefore, there is no actual evidence that evolution has occurred either in the past or is occurring in the present.[56] As we discussed in the previous chapter, there is a false reading of the hierarchy of being resulting in a misinterpretation which asserts that there are causal links between various species within the hierarchy of being. A causal link requires actual evidence and this evidence has been wanting. Other areas of study which have been ignored by many of those supporting evolution have been the area of stratification and sedimentology,[57] paleontology,[58] genetic entropy[59] and irreducibly complex biological systems.[60] Any theory or hypothesis

---

contrary to evolution.

[56] Johnson, *Darwin on Trial*, p. 50 observes: "...[one of] the outstanding characteristics of the fossil record is the absence of evidence for evolution." The entire chapter of Johnson's book deals with this issue.

[57] See Berthault, *Sedimentological Interpretation of the Tonto Group Stratigraphy (Grand Canyon Colorado River)*.

[58] See Johnson, op. cit.

[59] See Sanford, *Genetic Entropy and the Mystery of the Genome*.

[60] Behe, *Darwin's Black Box*, passim.

to be seriously considered must take into consideration all of the evidence. This has become a fundamental problem for evolutionary theory since very often it must ignore certain kinds of evidence. Any true explanation of nature must include *all* of the evidence; otherwise, the theory or hypothesis, as it stands, is unfounded. Furthermore, "an hypothesis must be probable (not in conflict with other truths and not leading to consequences against the facts), useful (as guiding and suggesting further research and experiment), and capable of being further tested" (Princ. 261) and "no argument or conclusion contrary to the evident facts is valid." (Princ. 289) Conversely, we may say, "an hypothesis or explanation which contradicts evident facts is not rationally tenable." (Princ. 290)

1. **The principle of economy**:
A. An explanation that accounts for all the facts in terms of a single or a few principles is preferable to the more complex theory. (Princ. 292A)

One of the problems with evolution is that it ends up multiplying causes without a sufficient reason. In other words, the evolutionist ends up having to assert that a number of different mutations must occur in order for something to reach a stage where it is actually useful to a particular creature that displays the change for which the mutations are ordered. Each mutation must come generally from a different cause or from the same cause on a number of different occasions and this itself multiplies the number of principles and makes the theory more complex when we could simply say that God created the thing immediately.

B. An explanation of any phenomenon is to be regarded as better and truer in which the minimum number of factors, the fewer steps in the process, and more immediate causes are included. (Princ. 292A continued)

This variant of the principle of economy connects with what we stated immediately above in a more explicit way. Since in some theories of evolution there are millions of years required to gradually produce a particular set of characteristics in a particular living thing, steps are added in a process which are not necessary to postulate in order to give an adequate explanation.[61] Sometimes this principle is stated in the

---

[61]This theory of evolution is contrary to another theory of evolution called punctuated equilibrium. Punctuated equilibrium is a theory in evolutionary biology which proposes that most reproducing species will experience little evolutionary change for most of their geological history, remaining in a stasis which is broken up by rare and rapid events of branching speciation in which

form of: "in an explanation, one is not to multiply causes without a sufficient reason." Following this formulation, we can see how creation constitutes a more perfect fulfillment of the principle of economy than does any theory of evolution. This is because God suffices to account as the primary causal principle of the whole of creation.[62] This would indicate that even though God

species split into two or multiple distinct species, rather than one species gradually transforming into another. Punctuated equilibrium is commonly contrasted with the theory of phyletic gradualism, which proposes that evolution generally occurs uniformly and by the steady and gradual transformation of whole lineages. In other words, evolution is a generally smooth and continuous process. In 1972, Niles Eldredge and Stephen Jay Gould published a paper developing this theory and proposed that the degree of gradualism commonly attributed to Charles Darwin is virtually nonexistent in the fossil record, and that stasis dominates the history of most fossil species. Even if it is held that punctuated equilibrium does not violate the principle of economy, it still would violate the other principles discussed earlier. This also brings to the fore the fact that even among evolutionists themselves, there is not unanimity in relationship to the theory behind evolution.

[62]That this is not just a *deus ex machina* explanation, read below in relationship to the creation of substances.

often uses secondary causes to bring about certain things, this is in the order of accidents rather than substances. Since a species pertains to substances having the same essence, we can see how God immediately creating each species by creating individuals within that species fulfills the principle of economy more perfectly than any evolutionary theory.

Nor is it necessary to appeal to any kind of revelation in order to actually come to this conclusion. For the Scholastics, St. Thomas being preeminent among them, every essence is immediately created by God and could not be caused by any created substance.[63] The essential reason for this is that to create a substance requires the ability to bridge the gap between nothing and something. The gap between nothing and something that is being actualized requires an infinite power since the ontological distance between nothing and something is infinite. This requires a being of infinite power and therefore can only pertain to God, since every created substance is not infinite but finite according to its mode of being. Therefore it is impossible to state that a created thing can be the cause of a new species.

C. In identifying an unseen cause of a phenomenon, the least cause capable of

---

[63]See ST I, q. 45, a. 5 and De pot., q. 3, a. 4, among the numerous places St. Thomas says this.

explaining the phenomenon must be accepted. In other words, a proportionate cause is required and suffices. For example: miracles must not be postulated as an explanation of an event when a natural cause suffices in the circumstances.

Variant: a demonstration of the necessary truth of some unseen cause, reason, or theory requires both proof of the necessity and the suitability of the explanation offered and the exclusion of the other attempted explanations. (Princ. 292B)

It is here that we begin to realize that theistic evolution has difficulties. In this case, we run up against a bit of a problem in the literature. Some theistic evolutionists hold that evolution is just a natural process used by God to bring about the various forms of life. Other theistic evolutionists hold that evolution is a case of constant miracles being used in order to bring about the various forms of life. As to those who hold it is a natural process, they introduce God into the issue to provide what might be lacking in the order of nature, such as the order that one finds in the universe, which may not be accounted for by purely natural causes and this introduces the above philosophical difficulty where only God can create a substance as well as a whole host of other difficulties. Some theistic evolutionists may even be motivated by religious reasons in order to give credibility to the Scriptures or to make sure that God is not completely excluded, as we see in the case of theistic evolutionary theory.

Theistic evolution in this sense succumbs to different difficulties. If it is a natural process used by God, then all of the above violations of principle would likewise apply in this case. If God is used to supply on the side of the principle of sufficient reason, it ends up violating the principle of economy because God must intervene to supply the sufficient reason at each step. This indicates that it is not strictly a natural process but requires the introduction of God into each step to be able to achieve the next higher species in the evolutionary process. This violates the principle of economy because what is ultimately being stated is that nature does not suffice in order to produce each individual species on its own. This is a true enough principle but theistic evolution requires God to be involved in each individual step since the laws of nature do not suffice. At each step, therefore, God must suspend the laws of nature and add what is lacking in the order of nature. The definition of a miracle is: "something occurring aside the whole created nature".[64] Theistic evolution, whether it states that it is a natural process, which is really just a covert way of introducing constant miracles, or asserts outright that

---

[64]ST I, q. 110, a. 4: aliqua fiunt praeter ordinem totius naturae creatae. This would include the laws of nature and so one may say that a miracle is a suspension of the law(s) of nature. See also SCG III, c. 103.

miracles are constantly necessary for the process, violates the principle of economy. It violates the principle of economy because it posits a number of causes, in this case God intervening as a cause on repeated occasions, without a sufficient reason. In this sense, God creating directly all of the individual species in a short period of time without a large number of secondary causes more perfectly fulfills the principle of economy than any theory of evolution, theistic evolution included.

We already know that God must be part of this on a purely metaphysical level since to go from nothing to something requires an infinite power. Regardless of whether one holds to the Aristotelian theory that the world has always existed, or whether one holds to what we know by revelation that God created these things out of nothing from the beginning, does not matter as it pertains to this particular issue. While we know from revelation that God did create everything *ex nihilo*, St. Thomas points out that even if one holds that the world always existed, God still has to be the cause in relationship to essences which come into existence through substantial causation.[65]

---

[65]See above.

Conclusion

When we consider first philosophy, that is that branch of metaphysics which studies first principles, and we apply first principles to evolutionary theory, we begin to realize that every form of evolutionary theory violates some first principle(s). There are numerous other first principles which we did not consider in this small work, even though they equally could be considered in light of evolutionary theory. Our chief concern has been to show that, given some of the more evident first principles, it becomes clear that evolutionary theory is not able to be sustained rationally. Since it is irrational or contrary to reason to violate first principles in one's reasoning process, we can say that evolutionary theory is irrational or contrary to reason. While it is true that evolutionary theory is irrational, we should not think that everybody who holds evolutionary theory is intentionally being irrational, or that they would have sufficient knowledge of the first principles to recognize that their theory is irrational. However, in light of this study, in light of the findings of serious empirical research that contradicts the claims of the evolutionary hypothesis, and in light of theological considerations, it is our hope that the scientific and academic communities will stop taking a prejudiced view of the matter and begin considering the issue with greater intellectual clarity.

An Initial Dictionary of Scholastic Terms and Principles

This dictionary is obviously not meant to be exhaustive, but is intended primarily for those who do not have an extensive background in philosophical studies.

Abstraction: the process by which one proceeds from particulars to universals; to separate a part from the whole; an operation performed by the Agent Intellect in which it draws out the essence or concept latent in the Phantasm, i.e. an operation in which the Agent Intellect makes explicit to the Possible Intellect the Essence implicit in the Phantasm in the Passive Intellect.

Accident: that which does not exist of itself but in another as in a subject; refers to the last nine of the ten Categories of Aristotle.

Act: in Ontology, it refers to the existence of a thing.

Act, Pure: lacking any admixture of potency (ascribed only to God).

Agent: in Ethics, it refers to he who acts; in Ontology, it refers to that which causes.

Agere Sequitur Esse: Act (or operation) follows being; as a thing is so it acts; the mode of being determines the mode of operation; everything acts according to its nature in act.

Argument: a course of reasoning aimed at demonstrating the truth or falsity of something; sometimes used as a synonym of Syllogism.

Attribute: that quality which benefits a thing in a peculiar and original manner, so that, if other things share in it, it befits that thing above all and for the most part; a perfection naturally needed or present in a thing; something which belongs to or is predicable of a thing which is not accidental but essentially belongs to the thing; sometimes refers to the proper accident of a thing which does not enter into its definition.

Being: (1) a thing which exists; (2) the act of existence.

Body: the material element in a composite living thing.

Categories: the predicate of a proposition; one of the modes of being that may be asserted in predication, which are Substance, Quantity, Quality, Relation, Place, Time, Habit, Disposition, Action and Passion.

Cause: that upon which something depends for its existence or for its coming to be.

Cause, Efficient: that which causes the existence of a thing.

Cause, Final: the reason for which a thing is made.

Cause, First: that cause to which the effect is primarily and principally ascribed; usually refers to God; counter-distinguished from Second Cause.

Cause, Formal: the essence determining the creation of the thing

Cause, Second: that cause to which the effect is only secondarily ascribed; usually refers to a creature in relation to God as First Cause; counter-distinguished from First Cause.

Change: the process by which one thing becomes another; a transition from one form of existence to another.

Circumstances: those which are said to stand around a thing and are not essential to it.

Composite: a being which is made up of more than one part or element.

Contingent: that which can be otherwise.

Corruption: the going out of existence of a thing; in a substantial change, the one substance that goes out of existence is said to corrupt; counter-distinguished from Generation.

Create: to bring about the existence of a thing from nothing, i.e. to cause the existence of a thing out of nothingness; proper only to God; counter-distinguished from "Making."

Deduction: a form of logical reasoning in which the conclusion necessarily follows from the premises; a form of argumentation in which one proceeds from the general to the particular.

Definition: an oral or written expression of the essence of a thing.

Dependence: when the cause ceases to act or be, the effect ceases to be insofar as it is dependent on the influence of that cause.

Disposition: the ability to effect or suffer something; the innate readiness of something for certain kinds of activity.

Distinct: when one thing is not another.

Effect: that which depends upon something for its existence or for its coming to be.

Empiricism: a philosophical system or epistemology which asserts that man only has sense knowledge of reality.

End: that toward which something aims; that toward which something is ordered or directed.

Essence: what a thing is; that by which a thing is what it is.

Existence: the actuality of a thing; the perfection by means of which something is an existent; that by which something is.

Existent: that which has existence; that which exists.

Faculty: a potentiality or power of the soul by which it acts; a proper accident flowing from the essence of the soul by which it acts.

Finite: that which has boundary, limit or end.

First Philosophy: a branch of Metaphysics which studies the First Principles or Causes of things. **Form, Accidental**: that which confers a sort of secondary being on a substance already constituted in its proper species and determines it in one or an other accidental mode; the external shape, the outline, the figure, the visible structure of a body;

Form, Substantial: the constitutive element of a substance which is the principle or source of its activity and which determines its membership in a definite species or class; that which makes matter into a certain kind of being, e.g. the form of dogness makes this matter be a dog; the intelligible structure, characters constituting a substance or species of substances, as distinguished from the matter in which these characters are embodied.

Generation: the coming into existence of a thing; in a substantial change, the substance that comes into existence is said to be generated; counter-distinguished from Corruption.

Genus: that part of the essence of anything which belongs also to other things differing from it in Species; a class of objects possessing an identical character and consisting of two or more subclasses or species; counter distinguished from Species.

Hypothesis: see Postulate.

Hierarchy of Being: the ontological order from the greatest to the least existing things.

Induction: a form of philosophical reasoning in which the conclusion does not necessarily follow from the premises, the certainty of the conclusion is based upon the amount of

support provided by the premises; a form of argumentation in which one proceeds from the particular to the general.
Inference: in Logic, the procedure by which one derives the conclusion from the premises.
Infinite: that which has no limit, boundary or end; counter-distinguished from the Finite.
Intellect: the faculty by which a spiritual substance knows.
Intellect, Agent: an immaterial part of the intellect of man which abstracts the essence of a thing
from a given phantasm.
Intellect, Possible: the immaterial part of the faculty in man by which he knows; this faculty performs three acts: (1) Simple Apprehension, (2) Judgment and (3) Ratiocination.
Law: a promulgated ordinance of reason with respect to the common good, by him who has care of the community (ST I-II, 90, 4 - quaedam rationis ordinatio ad bonum commune, ab eo qui curam communitatis habet, promulgata).
Logic: the philosophical science and art of right reasoning.
Make: the bringing about (causing) of a thing from something pre-existing; counter-distinguished from Create.
Matter: that out of which something is made; the passive element in Change; the substrate of substantial Change.
Metaphysics: a philosophical science which studies being and its attributes; metaphysics is broken into three branches: (1) First Philosophy, (2) Ontology (sometimes called metaphysics in the more restrictive sense) and (3) Natural Theology.
Motion: the reduction of a thing from potency, insofar as it is in potency, to act.
Nature: the essence of a thing as it is a principle of motion or action.
Necessary: that which cannot be otherwise.

Non Sequitur: a conclusion which does not follow from its premises.

Perfection: the state of being complete; a state in which a thing possesses all the goods proper to it. **Philosophy**: Love of Wisdom; the science which studies the essences of things.

Postulate: a primary truth of a given branch of knowledge, but which is derived from another branch of knowledge; a postulate which is not certain or not evident from another branch of knowledge or not evident in itself is known as a hypothesis.

Potency: that which is capable of being actualized; sometimes used in the same sense as Faculty. **Power**: see Faculty.

Premise: a statement or Proposition used in support of a Conclusion.

Principle: that from which any thing in any way proceeds; the starting point of being, change or thought.

Principle, First: a principle which does not proceed from a prior principle in its own series.

Principle, Logical: a truth from which other truths proceed, i.e. a principle of knowledge; a logical principle may be expressed in (a) an ontological formula, then a general truth or a definition is expressed in terms of being; (b) a logical formula, then a general truth or proposition is expressed in terms of thought or speech (that is, of affirmation, negation, or predication). The philosophical principles of thought in scholasticism are usually principles ABOUT real beings.

Principle, Ontological: a being from which another proceeds.

Principle, Practical: a principle concerned with activity, whether doing or making.

Principle, Real: see principle, ontological.

Principle, Self-Evident: a principle which is immediately known, i.e. one which is seen to be true without reasoning or deduction from other principles.

Principle, Speculative: a principle concerned with truth for its own sake.

Priority: when one thing is before another, either in the order of being, time, causality or thought.

Property: a characteristic feature of a thing; an accident essential to and common to all members of a class or species; an attribute that does not form part of the essence of its subject but necessarily results from that essence as a formal effect; a characteristic trait or attribute of a class of things.

Proposition: an assertion which affirms or denies something; the product of the second act of the intellect, viz. Judgment.

Quality: that by virtue of which a thing is such and such; one of the ten Categories.

Quantity: how much; the magnitude of a thing; the amount; one of the ten Categories.

Rationalism: a philosophical system in which the criterion of truth is not sensory but intellectual and deductive, i.e. the criterion for truth is reason and not reality.

Realism: the epistemological position which holds that man can have true intellectual knowledge of things.

Realism, Moderate: a form of realism which holds that we can have true intellectual knowledge by means of the senses.

Realism, Radical: a form of realism which does not distinguish between reality and the thing known.

Reason: the intellectual principle in man by which man knows; the Intellect.

Relation: the reference of one thing to another; those things are called relative, which, being either said to be *of* something else or *related* to something else, are explained by reference to that other thing; one of the ten Categories.

Relation, Causal: a Real Relation between two things which exists by virtue of the fact that one of the things causes the existence of the other.

Relation of Reason: a Relation between two things which only exists in the mind of the knower and not in the things themselves.

Relation, Real: a Relation which actually exists in reality between two things.

Science: an organized body of knowledge; knowledge of something through its causes; the intellectual virtue, residing in the intellect, by which one judges rightly (i.e. it corrects the second act of the intellect of judgment) about the things of this world; the Gift of the Holy Spirit, residing in the intellect, by which we judge the things of this world the way God judges them.

Self-Evident: that which is immediately known; what is self-evident is prior to and not capable of proof.

Simple: that which is not composed of parts.

Species: the subdivision of a Genus constituted by the specific difference; common Nature or Essence; counter-distinguished from Genus.

Subject: in the ontological order, that upon which accidental determinations depend for existence, or that in which forms are received; in the logical order, that of which something is predicated; synonym of Supposit, Hypostasis and Substance.

Substance: that which exists of itself and not in another as in a subject.

Syllogism: a logical argument in which a Conclusion is inferred from a Major Premise and a Minor Premise.

Theology, Natural: the branch of Metaphysics which has as its object of study God, His Attributes, Separated Substances and Creation as they can be known through the natural light of reason.

Theology, Revealed: the sacred science, which by the light of faith, studies the deposit of faith, i.e. that which has been revealed by God.

Truth: the adequation of the intellect and thing ("adequatio intellectus et rei"); the congruity between what is in the intellect or mind of the knower and the thing known as it exists in reality.

Bibliography

Aristotle, *The Basic Works of Aristotle*. Richard McKeon, ed.
Random House. New York. 1941. Behe, Michael J., *Darwin's
Black Box : the Biochemical Challenge to Evolution.* Simon
and
    Schuster. New York, 1998.
Berthault, Guy. "Sedimentological Interpretation of the Tonto
Group Stratigraphy (Grand Canyon
    Colorado River)". *Lithology and Mineral Resources*,
Russian Academy of Science. vol.39.
    No. 5, 2004.
    Deferrari, Roy, J., ed. *A Latin-English Dictionary of*
    St. Thomas Aquinas. St. Paul Editions. Boston.
Gardeil, H.D. *Introduction to the Philosophy of St. Thomas
Aquinas: Metaphysics*. B. Herder Book Co. St. Louis,
Missouri. 1967. John Paul II, *Fides et Ratio*, 1998.
Johnson, Phillip. *Darwin on Trial*. Washington, D.C..
Regnery Gateway.1991.
Leo XIII. *Aeterni Patris*. Rome. 1879.
McInerny, D. Q. *Metaphysics*. The Priestly Fraternity of St.
Peter. Elmhurst, Pennsylvania. 2004. Pius X. *Pascendi
Dominici Gregis*. Rome. 1907.
    Ripperger, Chad. *An Introduction to the Science of*
    Mental Health. Sensus Traditionis Press. Denton, NE.
    2007.
Sacred Congregation For Catholic Education, *Ratio
Fundamentalis*, 1980.
Sanford, John C. *Genetic Entropy and the Mystery of the
Genome*. Ivan Press. 2005.

Thomas Aquinas. *Thomae Aquinatis Opera Omnia.*
Iussu Impensaque Leonis XIII, edita. Roma: ex
Typographia Polyglotta et al. 1882.
----------------------. *Summa Contra Gentiles.* trans. Anton
Pegis. University of Notre Dame Press.
Wuellner, Bernard. *A Dictionary of Scholastic Philosophy.*
The Bruce Publishing Company.
Milwaukee. 1966.
----------------------. *Summary of Scholastic Principles.* Loyola
University Press. Chicago. 1956.

CPSIA information can be obtained
at www.ICGtesting.com
Printed in the USA
BVOW11s1030110518
515762BV00002B/175/P